Just a little
more pear-aphanalia!
mom
2012

FAMOUS PAIRS

ARIEL BOOKS

**Andrews McMeel
Publishing**
Kansas City

FAMOUS PAIRS

A DELICIOUSLY ABSURD COLLECTION OF PORTRAITS

JEANNIE SPRECHER

WITH KIM O'BRIEN

ISBN-13: 978-0-7407-5493-7
ISBN-10: 0-7407-5493-9
Library of Congress
Control Number: 2005924873

MANY THANKS TO

Kim O'Brien, whose unnatural wit and natural (albeit bizarre) talent in pear styling helped bring this book to life. / Armand Eisen of Ariel Books for his truly uncontainable enthusiasm for this project (which led to numerous pre-dawn "pair idea that can't wait!" phone calls that I hope will now cease). / Family and friends for living, breathing, talking, and eating pears beyond reason. / And finally, the Pear Actor's Guild (PAG), without whose cooperation and lax standards this book would not have been possible.

: V

"SECURITY TO
PRODUCE!"

IT ALL STARTED about a year ago. I went to my local Ralph's to pick up a few staples: milk, aspirin, Double Stuf Oreos. While ducking through the produce section my shopping stamina waned, so I stopped to open my box of cookies in front of a giant pear display. I became mesmerized by the different colors and shapes, and before I could avert my eyes (this you'll find hard to believe), the pears started pairing up.

Was that Fred Astaire dipping Ginger Rogers in the Bosc bin? Bonnie and Clyde? Bill and Monica? (Ew.) I just stood dumbstruck—and starstruck—washing down the last of my cookies with a gallon of milk.

I immediately called my friend Kim. "Get down here! The fruit is dancing and my cookies are gone!" God love her, she came right away, and God commit her, she saw what I saw.

And that's how it happened. That's how FAMOUS PAIRS got its roots.

Seventeen produce departments, a dozen run-ins with super-scary grocery store security, and four sticky hands later, our casting was complete.

Yes, we'd heard the warnings about working with puppies, children, and famous produce, but we're happy to report no major incidents. There were the expected complaints: don't shoot my bad side, the camera adds ten ounces, don't light me on fire. . . . Celebs. God's gift, huh? *(See Adam and Eve, page 19.)*

Happily we all survived. Except for our models (a girl's gotta eat). And we're now proud to present to you this fresh look at the most famous pairs in history. BON APPÉTIT.

FAMOUS PAIRS

MIKE TYSON AND EVANDER HOLYFIELD

ANNA NICOLE SMITH AND J. HOWARD MARSHALL II

DOLLY PARTON

AMERICAN GOTHIC

BONNIE AND CLYDE

YIN AND YANG

BILL AND MONICA

KING HENRY VIII AND ANNE BOLEYN

ADAM AND EVE

MADONNA AND CHILD

DUDLEY DO-RIGHT AND PENELOPE PITSTOP

FRED ASTAIRE AND GINGER ROGERS

BUFFY AND THE VAMPIRE

HANNIBAL LECTER AND AN OLD FRIEND

PICASSO AND MARIE-THERESE WALTER

DR. FRANKENSTEIN AND THE MONSTER

LAUREL AND HARDY

DAVID COPPERFIELD AND HIS LOVELY ASSISTANT

HARRY AND BESS HOUDINI

ANDY WARHOL AND MARILYN MONROE

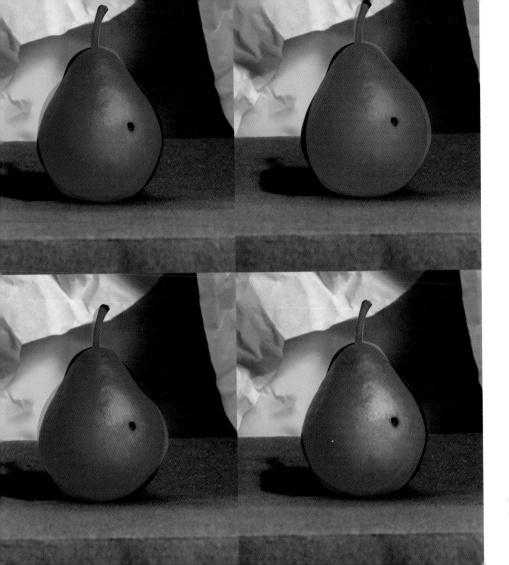

S AND M

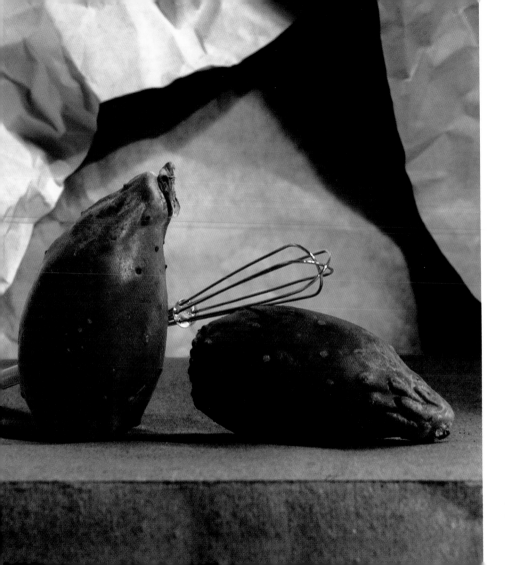

MICHAEL JACKSON, THEN AND NOW

SID AND NANCY

MARY POPPINS AND BERT THE CHIMNEY SWEEP

CHANG AND ENG

FIRE AND ICE

WILE E. COYOTE AND THE ROADRUNNER

MATADOR AND BULL

STOP AND GO

TART AND VICAR

DR. JEKYLL AND MR. HYDE

DR. EVIL AND MINI ME

LOT AND HIS WIFE

DALAI LAMA AND NOTHINGNESS

NO PEARS WERE HARMED IN THE MAKING OF THIS BOOK
except for those that were burned, shot, stabbed, frozen,
splayed, skinned, mashed, dropped, and eaten alive.

Photography, book design, and photo post-production:
JEANNIE SPRECHER

Concepts, casting, and pear styling:
JEANNIE SPRECHER AND KIM O'BRIEN

DESIGNER'S NOTES

FAMOUS PAIRS was designed and produced on a Mac (of course),
using Quark, Photoshop, and aspirin. It was typeset using Trade Gothic,
CorporateEBSK, and Clarendon fonts. Photos were shot with a Nikon D100.
Pears were purchased primarily at Ralph's.